A ROOKIE BIOGRAPHY

JOHN PHILIP SOUSA

The March King

By Carol Greene

CHILDRENS PRESS ®

CHICAGO

This book is for Meghan Birdsong.

John Philip Sousa (1854-1932)

Library of Congress Cataloging-in-Publication Data

Greene, Carol.
    John Philip Sousa, the march king / by Carol Greene.
       p. cm. — (A Rookie biography)
    Summary: A simple biography of the famous band leader and composer
who was known as the March King.
    ISBN 0-516-04226-2
    1. Sousa, John Philip, 1854-1932—Juvenile literature. 2. Composers—
United States—Biography—Juvenile literature. [1. Sousa, John Philip,
1854-1932. 2. Composers. 3. Musicians.] I. Title. II. Title: John Philip
Sousa. III. Series: Greene, Carol. Rookie biography.
M13930.S7G7 1992
784 8'4'092—dc20
  [B]   91-37891
                                            CIP
                                      AC MN

John Philip Sousa
was a real person.
He was born in 1854.
He died in 1932.
Sousa led many bands
and wrote many marches.
This is his story.

TABLE OF CONTENTS

Military bands wore uniforms like these during the Civil War.

Chapter 1

Bands and More Bands

Thump, thump,
thump, thump!

The sound of bands filled
the air in Washington, D.C.,
when John Philip Sousa
was a little boy.
Soon the United States would
be fighting the Civil War.

John's father played in
the United States Marine Band.
No wonder John wanted to be
a musician when he grew up.

Many years after the doughnut problem, this picture was taken of John and his mother.

But he almost didn't
grow up at all.

One day, when he was 5,
John's mother wouldn't give
him any more doughnuts.

"You'll be sorry," said John.

He went outside.
Cold rain poured down.
But John lay on a board
in the rain for half an hour.
Then his mother found him.

John got so sick
that he almost died.
He had to stay home
for two long years.
Now *he* was the sorry one.

While John was home,
his father and sister taught
him to read and write.
Then, when he was 7,
he went to a nearby school.
He went to music school, too.

John learned
to play many
instruments,
including the
harp, which
he played
throughout
his life.

John learned to play the violin
and other instruments.
He was very good at music.
When he was 11, he even
started his own dance band.
The other players were adults.

Then one day, a man told John
he should run away from home
and join a circus band.

"A circus band!" thought John.
"How exciting that would be!"

"Come to the circus grounds
tomorrow night," said the man.

"All right," said John.

But John's father found
out about John's plans.
The next morning,
he woke John up.

United States Marines in 1862

"Put on your Sunday clothes,"
he told John.

After breakfast, he and John
went to the Marine offices.

"Sign here," said John's father.

John signed.
There would be
no circus
for John Sousa.
He was a Marine
in the Marine Band.
And he was only 13!

A group of Marines marches by the Marine Barracks in Washington, D.C., in 1861.

Chapter 2

Love Stories

John went to school
while he was a Marine.
He studied more music, too.

During the day, he played
in the Marine Band.
In the evening, he played
with other orchestras.
He taught children music
and wrote music himself.

One day, a friend asked
John to write some music
for a young lady.
The friend wanted to
please the young lady.
So John wrote some dances.

They were not great.
But John went on writing.

When he was 20, John
left the Marine Band.
He also fell in love
with a girl called Emma.

"You can't marry Emma,"
said Emma's father.
"Musicians are too poor."

"I'll go away for two years
and make money," said John.
"Then I'll come back
and marry Emma."

John Philip Sousa at age 19

So John traveled around
with different orchestras.
He ended up in Philadelphia.
Two years later, he saw Emma.
She was dating someone else.
John gave up on her.

But he went on playing
and writing music.
In 1879, he became head of
a group that did shows.
A young girl called Jennie
sang with this group.

"I liked everything
about her," said John later.

John and Jennie Sousa. This photo
was taken shortly before his death.

In fact, he fell in love
with Jennie and on
December 30, 1879,
they were married.

"Like all good love stories,"
John wrote later,
"we lived happily ever after."

John and Jennie (left) with one of their daughters

Chapter 3

Leader of the Band

Before long, John and Jennie
had three children:
John Philip, Jr.,
Jane, and Helen.
John had a new job, too.

John (right) with his son John, Jr., and grandson, John III

In England, King Edward VII decorated John with the Victorian Order.

In 1880, the Marine Band
asked him to be their leader.
Of course, John said yes.
He moved his family
back to Washington, D.C.

First John had to work
to make the band better.
He found better music
and better musicians.
He made the band
practice for hours.
And he wrote marches.

The Marine Band in 1890

John leads the Marine Band in "The Stars and Stripes Forever" at the White House while President Herbert Hoover (right, on bottom stair) looks on.

On Saturdays, the Marine Band
played by the White House.
On Wednesdays, they played
at the Marine Barracks.
On Thursdays, they played
at the Capitol.

The band played well.
Soon big crowds came
to all their concerts.
They heard many
of John's marches.

The sheet music for "Semper Fidelis" (above).
John wore white gloves when he led the band.

The "Semper Fidelis" march took its name from the Marine motto. (*Semper Fidelis* means "always faithful.")

The "Washington Post" march was named for the newspaper that asked John to write it.

The phonograph was invented by Thomas Edison.
Early models had a trumpet-like speaker and played wax tubes.

John wrote many other
kinds of music, too.
But it was his marches
that made him famous.
People began to call him
"the March King."

Back then, the phonograph
was a new invention.
It played wax tubes
instead of records.

John and the Marine Band made many wax tubes of their marches. People loved them.

In 1891, one of John's dreams
for the band came true.
They took a trip
and played for people
in New England
and the Midwest.

John got sick after that trip.
He and Jennie went to Europe
so he could rest.
But soon he was back
and ready for another trip—
all the way to the West Coast.

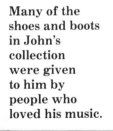

Many of the shoes and boots in John's collection were given to him by people who loved his music.

Then, in 1892,
a man told John
he should start
his own band.
That sounded
good to John.

Chapter 4

Around the World

Soon, the Sousa Band
was ready to go.
Many fine players joined.
They wanted to work with John.

The Sousa Band made
its home in New York City.
But John took the band
on trips, lots of trips.

John wrote many marches
for his band, too.
In 1896, he and Jennie
were on a boat,
traveling from Europe
to the United States.

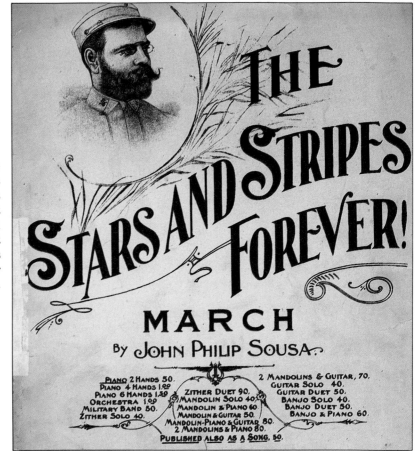

All at once, John heard a band
playing in his brain.
"It kept on," he said,
"playing, playing, playing."

When John got home,
he wrote down the music
his "brain-band" had played.
It was his greatest march,
"The Stars and Stripes Forever."

**The Sousa Band playing "The Stars and Stripes Forever"
at the Paris Exposition in 1900**

In 1900, John took
the Sousa Band to Europe.
They played 175 concerts.
The people in Europe
loved them and they
went back again and again.

When not leading
his band or
writing marches,
John loved to ride
his favorite horse,
Patrician Charlie.

Back home, John fought for
a new law for composers.
He said they should be paid
when their music was recorded.
John and others won that fight.

In 1910, the Sousa Band
took a trip around the world.
It lasted one year,
one month, and one week.

John leads the Sousa Band in 1916. Soon after,
the United States entered World War I.

John could have gone on
with his band
and his trips forever.
But in 1917,
everything changed.

The United States
entered World War I.

John led the Navy Band in 1917.

Chapter 5

The March King

꠸꠸꠸꠸꠸꠸꠸꠸꠸꠸꠸꠸꠸꠸꠸꠸꠸꠸꠸꠸꠸꠸꠸꠸꠸꠸꠸꠸꠸꠸꠸꠸꠸꠸꠸

"We need you to train
young players in our band,"
the U.S. Navy told John.
"Will you do it?"

"I won't fail you," said John.
"I'm past 62, but you'll find
me a healthy fellow."

So he joined the
Navy and started
a new band.
They played
on ships.
And they gave
concerts to
raise money
for the war.
They sold
more than
21 million dollars
of war bonds.

John and his World War I Navy Band

Left: John Philip Sousa
dressed as Santa Claus
to help raise money for
the poor. Center: Sousa
prepares to lead the
band in a radio concert.
Bottom: Three famous
American writers of music—
(left to right) Victor Herbert,
Irving Berlin, and
John Philip Sousa.

The Sousa Band performed at the New York Hippodrome Theater in 1922.

After the war, John went
back to his Sousa Band.
During the 1920s, they
played all over America.
And John wrote more marches.

By then, people everywhere
loved John and his music.

Sousa was greeted at the train
station in Omaha, Nebraska, by
the band from Boys Town (above).
Sousa meets with a member of
Chicago's Senn High School band,
which won the Illinois high-school
band competition in 1927.

John helped school bands
and orchestras, too.
Children were some
of his biggest fans.

In 1926, John was in
Milwaukee on his birthday.
He was 72 that year.
So 72 children gave him
72 birthday cakes,
each with one candle.

John cuts the cake with a sword at his 77th birthday party

In 1931, when John was 77,
he had a huge birthday party
in New York City.
There was even a concert
on the radio for him.
It played only his music.

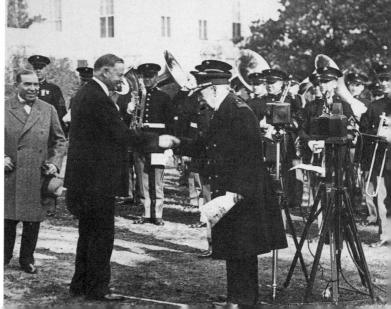

Sousa leads the world's
largest band (above).
Sousa and his former
Marine Band comrades
(right) played for
President Herbert Hoover at
the White House in 1930.

"I want to live to 100,"
John told his friends,
"and write more marches."

Early in 1932, John led the
Army, Navy, and Marine bands
together in one big concert.
They were celebrating
the 200th anniversary
of George Washington's birth.

A few days later,
he led the Marine
Band again.
That was John's
last concert.

John relaxing with his pet dogs (left) and writing a new march (right)

On March 4, he went to see
a friend in Pennsylvania.
He talked a lot about God.
John felt God helped him
write his music.

Two days later, John
died in his hotel room
in Reading, Pennsylvania.

The Marine
Band played
at Sousa's
grave in 1979
to mark
the 125th
anniversary of
Sousa's birth.

John was buried in
the Congressional Cemetery
in Washington, D.C.
People all over America
listened to his funeral
service on the radio.

John Philip Sousa's flag-draped coffin passes
through the streets of Washington, D.C.

Eight white horses
pulled the wagon
that carried John's body.
The Marine Band played
hymns and Sousa marches.

At the very end of the
service, one Marine
lifted his bugle
and played "Taps."

John Philip Sousa,
the man people called
The March King,
would have liked that.

Crowds of admirers pay their respects
at John Philip Sousa's funeral.

Important Dates

1854 November 6—Born in Washington, D.C., to Maria and John Sousa

1868 Joined the United States Marine Corps

1876 Went to Philadelphia

1879 Married Jane ("Jennie") Bellis

1880 Became leader of the U.S. Marine Band

1892 Started the Sousa Band

1896 Wrote "The Stars and Stripes Forever"

1910 Took the Sousa Band around the world

1917 Became leader of the U.S. Navy Band

1932 March 6—Died in Reading, Pennsylvania

INDEX

Page numbers in boldface type indicate illustrations.

ABOUT THE AUTHOR

Carol Greene has degrees in English literature and musicology. She has worked in international exchange programs, as an editor, and as a teacher of writing. She now lives in Webster Groves, Missouri, and writes full-time. She has published more than 100 books, including those in the Childrens Press Rookie Biographies series.